Tania 金

Veg Matters

forget the lentils

£2

Veg Matters

forget the lentils
just spoil yourself

Rose Elliot

With decorations by Trevor Newton

Little Books by Big Names™

First published in the United Kingdom in 2003 by Little Books Ltd,
48 Catherine Place, London SW1E 6HL

10 9 8 7 6 5 4 3 2 1

A CIP catalogue record for this book is available from the British Library.

ISBN: 1 904435 03 3

The author and publisher will be grateful for any information that will
assist them in keeping future editions up-to-date. Although all reasonable
care has been taken in the preparation of this book, neither the publisher, editors
nor the author can accept any liability for any consequences arising from the
use thereof, or the information contained therein.

*Many thanks to: Jamie Ambrose for editorial management and photographic
assistance, Eluned Jones for editorial assistance, Ghost for original jacket
styling and illustration, Mousemat Design for jacket and text design, Margaret
Campbell of Scan-Hi Digital and Craig Campbell of QSP Print for printing
consultancy, and Angie Hipkin for indexing. Printed and bound in Scotland
by Scotprint.*

CONTENTS

I

Healthy Feasts
for Busy People

It's late, you're tired, and you want to eat healthy vegetarian food. The last thing you need is to spend hours in the kitchen soaking lentils, but is there an alternative?

Yes, indeed – as the recipes in this book prove. Even if you're short of time, you can still indulge in good vegetarian food. You can spoil yourself and make fabulous meals with minimum fuss and maximum pleasure. What's more, you'll discover that meatless cooking is neither a chore nor a bore.

Unlike decades ago, when finding a variety of quality ingredients was difficult, today's markets and supermarkets offer a huge array of wonderful fresh vegetables and herbs, not to mention pasta, fruit, breads, spices and flavourings. Such ingredients are a far cry from the traditional 'rabbit-food' image of vegetarians. They make shopping a culinary adventure – and cooking an absolute joy. *Forget the Lentils* is designed to show you just how simple the latter is.

All the recipes included here are quick and easy to make. Some can be produced in a flash and set on the table in the blink of an eye. Others require a bit of gentle preparation, followed by a spell in the oven (or freezer) while you sit down and enjoy that well-deserved drink.

The best news is that you don't have to be a whizz in the kitchen to create these dishes. Even if you aren't a very experienced cook, or don't possess a huge amount of kitchen equipment, you can still prepare them with ease. Healthy and effortless – what more could you need?

And lest you think there's too much emphasis on 'health' here, let me give you a taste of what *I* mean by indulgence. Many of the dishes in this book use a range of exotic and exciting ingredients. Try Oven-baked Asparagus Frittata, for example, or Red and Gold Peppers with Feta and Cherry Tomatoes. Winter Roast Veg with Halloumi, and Fettucine with Pecorino Cream and Truffle Oil are both, I'm sure you'll agree, a far cry from the standard nut loaf or tofu burgers of vegetarian meals past.

I haven't neglected desserts, either, so you can round out your meal with such delights as Fast and Wonderful Chocolate Brownies or Ginger-baked Pears. Despite their sexy-sounding names, none of these recipes are time-consuming or intimidating to make, and fresh ingredients ensure that they are delicious. The point is to make something you enjoy, so relax and have fun.

In this modern world of hard work and equally hard play, you need to remember to spoil yourself in the kitchen and at the dining table more than ever. With this book, you can do that with ease – and eat healthily into the bargain.

2

The Golden Rules of Time-saving

To save time, it pays to have a quick check in your kitchen cupboard before you go shopping. Once you've got in the basic packets and jars, you can top them up as stocks get low; pick up some fresh produce, and you're ready to cook. The basics are listed below.

DRY GOODS

Chocolate
Keep a good dark one with 70 percent cocoa solids; also white chocolate for indulgent recipes such as White Chocolate Cheesecake on page 154.

Cornflour or arrowroot
I prefer arrowroot to cornflour and use it mixed with water instead of beaten egg for deep-frying. It gives a much crisper result.

Dried breadcrumbs
For coating fritters, use the natural, uncoloured ones.

Digestive biscuits
To make a base for cheesecakes and tortes.

Flour
Buy small bags of both plain and self-raising.

Nuts
Cashews, pine nuts and walnuts. For freshness, keep these in the freezer; they don't need thawing before use.

Pasta
Buy favourites such as spaghetti, rigatoni, penne, farfalle, fettucine, tagliatelle, linguine and pappardelle.

Porcini, dried
Useful for intensifying flavours in mushroom dishes.

Rice
Keep basmati (it cooks in only 10 minutes) on hand, as well as a risotto rice such as carnaroli or arborio.

Sugar
Caster has a mellower flavour. Light-brown sugar is sometimes useful for puddings.

Sun-dried or sun-blush tomatoes
Usually found in a packet near the porcini.

CONDIMENTS AND SPICES

Bay leaves
Improve with drying, so they're easy to keep on hand.

Bouillon powder
Try Marigold Vegetable Bouillon, now available in supermarkets as well as health shops. When I say 'stock' in a recipe, this is what I mean, dissolved in water.

Cardamom
Used only in one recipe in this book, but a lovely spice to have, and to use more often if you like it.

Chillies, chilli flakes
A jar of dried red chillies or red chilli flakes is handy.

Cinnamon
The powdered type.

Cumin or cumin seeds
Very useful for a store cupboard. I love the flavour, so it's in quite a few recipes.

Curry powder
A useful quick, spicy flavouring.

Nutmeg
Keep as ready-ground, but freshly grated nutmegs yield a better flavour.

Pepper
Buy spare black peppercorns for your grinder.

Saffron
I'm sure you can get it more cheaply if you have a Moroccan or Middle Eastern shop near you, but I usually buy a jar from the spice rack in the supermarket. It's fine – though expensive.

Salt
I like Maldon sea salt, which you can scrunch over food with your fingers.

Turmeric
Lovely in curries and so good for you, too! Studies have shown that turmeric benefits everything from blood sugar to liver function.

JARS AND BOTTLES
Artichoke hearts in oil
Great for adding to cooked pasta or salads.

Black olives
Buy loose at supermarket delis or Middle Eastern shops.

Capers
These come either salted or packed in vinegar. Rinse the salted ones thoroughly before use.

Cranberry sauce
Choose a nice fruity one.

Mayonnaise
Buy the best quality you can afford. Once opened, keep it in the fridge.

Olive oil
Aim for extra-virgin for salad dressings; a lighter type for shallow-frying (or use rape-seed oil: see page 16).

Sherry, Madeira and vermouth
Pretty interchangeable as far as these recipes are concerned. Keep a bottle of something fortified in the cupboard and you don't have to open a bottle of wine every time you make a risotto.

Stem ginger
The kind in syrup in a pretty jar, for some puddings.

Tabasco sauce
This is one of those magic ingredients that really perks things up.

Thai red curry paste
I've only found one type that's vegetarian; most have shrimp paste or other fishy ingredients in them, so do read the label. It keeps well in the fridge.

Truffle oil
In a small bottle, from good supermarkets. Gives a wonderful earthy, sexy flavour to pasta, potatoes or anything bland enough to take it.

Vegetable oil
Rape-seed is the best oil for deep-frying, as it's the most stable (and that means the healthiest) of all the oils at high temperatures.

Vinegar
Red-wine vinegar is a basic staple. I also like the lightness of rice vinegar, while cider vinegar tastes good and is traditionally supposed to have health-giving properties. Raspberry vinegar is also used in one of the recipes in this book, but you could substitute another vinegar.

CHILLED OR DAIRY

Butter
Buy organic, if possible.

Cream and yoghurt
Again, it's worth getting organic if you can.

Chilled pastry
From any supermarket. The ready-rolled kind makes life much easier.

Cheese

Buy according to the recipe and keep well-wrapped in the fridge. It's always useful to have some fresh Parmesan to hand. Vegetarian cheeses are marked as such, but plenty of others are vegetarian and don't advertise it. If in doubt, ask.

Eggs

Free-range, organic. Size isn't important as far as these recipes are concerned.

BREAD

If your freezer is big enough, it's useful to keep one or two different types in stock. Choose from a packet of pitta bread, a baguette or ficelle, or some nice Italian bread, as well as a basic loaf.

CANS

Coconut milk

Used in this book in a Thai curry. Buy organic coconut milk, if possible.

Condensed milk

Just for one very indulgent ice-cream recipe.

Tomatoes

Organic tomatoes have no added citric acid. It's useful to have whole and chopped ones, too.

FRESH PRODUCE

Most of this you'd buy according to what recipes you are planning to cook, but a few basics are always useful.

Chillies

I love the long, slim red ones that aren't too hot. They often come in packs, and I just put any leftovers in the freezer.

Garlic

An everyday essential. Buy juicy, plump bulbs.

Ginger

Keep a big chunk of this in the fridge. No need to peel; just wash and grate.

Herbs

Buy as required. I love having pots of them on the kitchen window-sill. They don't last long (one good salad, and that's it) but they look nice.

Lemons

I use lemon juice in some form nearly every day. A splash of fresh lemon juice will perk up any dish.

Onions

Along with garlic, onions are the flavouring ingredient I use for most dishes.

ESSENTIAL EQUIPMENT

Efficient equipment makes life easier. One huge time- and temper-saver is a really good knife. Try some out in a good kitchen shop and take advice.

My favourite everyday, all-purpose knife is a Sabatier with an 18-cm (seven-inch) blade. It's not stainless, so it's a curse to clean, but it does mean I can keep it sharp more easily.

To go with the knife, you need a good chopping board: big and thick. I have to have wood. And you'd be surprised how much you use a really good potato peeler. I like a swivel-bladed one with a handle that you can hold like a knife, though some people prefer chunkier ones.

You also need an efficient grater. I'm devoted to my 'box' grater, which has a sharp slicing edge and nice open holes, one large set for grating things like cheese and carrots, and some small ones for lemon rind or even garlic. You might also prefer two or three of the ultra-sharp Microplane graters which are some of the trendy, must-have gadgets of our day.

I think you can probably make all the recipes in this book without recourse to a food processor, though when I got mine some years ago, I wondered how I had ever managed without it. It does save time. But if you're buying one, opt for a decent make that's simple to use – but doesn't try to do too much. Whisking, for instance, is best done with an electric hand whisk (and they're surprisingly cheap). I must have become quite lazy, because I really love my electric lemon-squeezer, which sits on my work surface and produces juice at the touch of a cut lemon half.

Good pans are another essential, and here, you really get what you pay for. I prefer stainless steel. Wooden spoons, a good sieve, a colander, measuring spoons and a jug, and some scales should round out your basic equipment essentials.

Finally – and we're talking big stuff here – if you're getting a new fridge, be sure that it's a large one. In an ideal world, make it two.

If I had to choose between them, I'd rather have a large fridge and a small freezer. A big fridge really does save time, because it means you can buy all your fresh vegetables, herbs, cheese and so on for the week in one go and know they'll be as bright and perky on Friday evening as they were on Saturday when you put them in.

3

Mediterranean Veg

The recipes in this section use Mediterranean vegetables (red and gold peppers, tomatoes, garlic, olives, basil), or else it's the recipes themselves that originate from Mediterranean countries. Admittedly, including Fast, Flaky Leek Pie (page 34) and Gratin Dauphinoise (page 42) is stretching the definition, but they *are* French – and far too delicious to leave out.

I've also slipped in Garlic Bread (page 30). Some of this, hot from the oven, is an easy way of turning a simple dish of vegetables, such as Oven-baked Ratatouille (page 28), into a complete meal. You could also add some fluffy cooked couscous or basmati rice.

WARM NEW POTATO, CHERRY TOMATO AND ASPARAGUS SALAD

This dish is delectable when made in early summer with Jersey Royal potatoes, the first of the season's asparagus, and tiny, sweet, cherry tomatoes. Serve as a side dish or as a complete light meal with soft, creamy cheese, such as peppered Boursin, or perhaps goats cheese.

Serves 4

500 g or 1 lb 2 oz Jersey Royal or other
   new potatoes, washed
225-250 g or 8-9 oz bunch of asparagus
225-250 g or 8-9 oz cherry tomatoes, halved
2 tbsp of freshly squeezed lemon juice
1 tbsp olive oil
4 tbsp roughly torn basil
salt and freshly ground black pepper

METHOD

1 The potatoes need to be roughly the same size, so halve or quarter as necessary. Put into a saucepan, cover with water, bring to the boil, cover and leave to simmer for about 10 minutes, or until the potatoes are almost cooked.

2 Bend the asparagus until the hard, tough ends break off. Discard these. Wash the asparagus carefully, as it can harbour grit in the flower heads. Cut each spear into two or three pieces, discarding the flower heads.

3 Add the stems of asparagus to the pan of potatoes. Let them boil for a couple of minutes, then add the rest and cook for few more minutes, or until both the asparagus and the potatoes and tender but not at all soggy when pierced with a sharp knife.

4 Drain. Add the cherry tomatoes, lemon juice, oil, basil and salt and pepper to taste. Toss the salad and serve hot or warm. It also tastes great cold.

OVEN-BAKED RATATOUILLE

Made from vegetables that roast so well, ratatouille is a natural for the oven. Turn it into a meal by serving with garlic bread (see page 30) or some hot fluffy couscous and cheese to follow.

Serves 2-4
1 large onion (red or purple)
1 large courgette (or 2 or 3 small ones)
1 large aubergine
2 red peppers
4 garlic cloves, peeled and roughly chopped
juice of half a lemon
2 tbsp olive oil
salt and freshly ground black pepper
4 tomatoes, quartered
several sprigs of fresh basil

1 Preheat the oven to 200°C (400°F or gas mark 6).

2 Peel the onion and quarter. Trim the courgettes and aubergine and cut each into chunky pieces, about the same size as the onion pieces. Halve and deseed the peppers and cut into similar-sized pieces.

3 Put the vegetables and garlic in a roasting tray, sprinkle with lemon juice, oil, some salt and pepper, then mix until well-coated. Put into the oven and cook, uncovered, for 20 minutes.

4 Add the tomatoes and cook for a further 20 minutes. Then tear the basil over the top and serve.

GARLIC BREAD

Serves 4
125 g or 4^1/$_2$ oz soft butter
3-4 garlic cloves, crushed
1 large baguette

1 Preheat the oven to 200°C (400°F or gas mark 6).

2 Beat the butter with the garlic. Slice the baguette at 2.5-cm (one-inch) intervals, without cutting right through the bottom.

3 Pull back the pieces and spread the cut sides with the garlic butter. Put onto a baking tray and bake for 15 to 20 minutes until it's piping hot, crisp and oozing garlicky butter.

ALL-SEASON EASY GREEK SALAD WITH WARM PITTA BREAD

Bring back summer with this easy salad.

Serves 4
2-4 pitta breads
200 g or 7 oz feta cheese
450 g or 1 lb tomatoes
half a cucumber, peeled
2 large spring onions
juice of half a lemon
1 tsp white-wine vinegar or cider vinegar
1 handful of black olives
2 tbsp olive oil
freshly ground black pepper

1 Warm the pitta breads under the grill.

2 Meanwhile, slice the cheese, tomatoes and cucumber into even-sized pieces, slice the spring onions, and put all into a bowl with the lemon juice, vinegar, olives and oil.

3 Grind in a bit of pepper, toss gently and serve with warm bread.

GRATIN DAUPHINOISE

This recipe is an indulgence, but in my family it's our ultimate comfort food. You have to wait for it to cook, but once it's in the oven you can relax with a drink until it's done. I generally serve it as a main course with a leafy salad or Lemony Braised Vegetables (see page 66).

Serves 2-4
900 g or 2 lb potatoes, peeled
55 g or 2 oz butter
2 garlic cloves, crushed
salt and freshly ground black pepper
grated nutmeg
300 ml or 10fl oz double cream

METHOD

1 Preheat the oven to 200°C (400°F or gas mark 6).

2 Using a sharp knife, the slicing side of a grater or the slicing disc of a food processor, slice the potatoes as thinly as you can. Put the slices into a colander and rinse under the cold tap.

3 Mix the butter with the garlic and use half to grease a shallow casserole dish generously. Put in the potato slices, layering them as best you can and seasoning between the layers with salt, pepper and grated nutmeg.

4 Pour the double cream over the top of the potatoes, then fill the carton with water and pour that over, too.

5 Dot the rest of the garlic butter over the top and bake for about one-and-a-half hours, or until the potato can easily be pierced with a pointed knife and the top is golden brown. If the top gets too brown before the inside is tender, cover with foil.

OVEN-BAKED ASPARAGUS FRITTATA

Serves 4
1 onion, sliced
1 tbsp olive oil
1 bunch asparagus
8 free-range eggs, lightly beaten
salt and freshly ground black pepper
2 tbsp chopped parsley
225 g or 8 oz Parmesan, freshly grated

1 Preheat the oven to 180°C (350°F or gas mark 4).

2 In a covered saucepan, cook the onion in the oil for seven to 10 minutes, until tender but not browned.

3 Bend the asparagus stems, letting them break where they will. Discard the tough ends and wash the rest. Cut into 3-cm (one-and-a-quarter-inch) lengths. Cook the asparagus in a little boiling water for three to four minutes, or until just tender, then drain.

4 Put the onion and asparagus into a shallow casserole dish. Cover with half the cheese. Season the beaten eggs, mix in the parsley, and pour over. Sprinkle with remaining Parmesan and bake for 15 to 20 minutes, or until set.

RED AND GOLD PEPPERS STUFFED WITH FETA AND CHERRY TOMATOES

Serves 4
2 red peppers
2 gold peppers
450 g or 1 lb feta cheese, diced
125 g or 4 1/2 oz cherry tomatoes, halved
salt and freshly ground black pepper

1 Preheat the oven to 200°C (400°F or gas mark 6).

2 Cut the peppers in half through their stalks, then remove the seeds, leaving the stalks intact. Put them into a roasting tin or casserole dish.

3 Divide the feta cheese and cherry tomatoes equally into the pepper halves, and grind some pepper over. You could add a touch of salt, but the feta will supply lots.

4 Put into the oven and bake for about 40 minutes, or until the feta is golden brown and melting, and the peppers are browning a bit at the edges.

FAST, FLAKY LEEK PIE

Serves 4
900 g or 2 lb leeks
200 g or 7 oz crème fraîche
2 tbsp chopped parsley
salt and freshly ground black pepper
1 tsp grated nutmeg
packet of ready-rolled puff pastry
milk or beaten egg to glaze

1 Preheat the oven to 200°C (400°F or gas mark 6).

2 Fill a saucepan with 2.5 cm (one inch) of water and bring to the boil. Clean the leeks, and cut into 2.5-cm (one-inch) lengths.

3 Put the leeks into the boiling water, cover and cook for seven minutes or so, until they

are tender. Drain well in a colander, making sure you get rid of all the water, then mix the leeks with the crème fraîche, chopped parsley, salt, pepper and nutmeg.

4 Cut the pastry into two equal halves. Lay one on a lightly floured baking sheet and spread the leek mixture on it, leaving 1 cm (half an inch) clear all round.

5 Brush this rim with cold water, then put the other piece of pastry on top. Press the edges together very well.

6 Brush the top with milk or beaten egg to glaze, then prick several times with a fork. Bake for about 40 minutes, or until puffed up and golden.

RÖSTI

Serves 4
1 kg or 2 lb 4 oz waxy potatoes
  (such as Cara), unpeeled
salt and freshly ground black pepper
2 tbsp olive oil
55 g or 2 oz butter

1 Cover the potatoes in water and boil for 10 to 12 minutes to soften them slightly. Drain into a colander, rinse under cold water, then strip off the skin and grate the potatoes. Season well.

2 Heat one tablespoon of the olive oil and half the butter in a large frying pan. Put in the potato mixture and press down well.

3 Fry until the base is crisp and browned – about 10 minutes – then slide the rösti out onto a plate. Heat the remaining oil and butter in the frying pan, then fry the rösti on the other side for seven to eight minutes until crisp and golden.

ASPARAGUS WITH QUICK
HOLLANDAISE SAUCE

Serves 4
2 bunches of asparagus
125 g or 4¹/₂ oz butter, in chunks
2 free-range egg yolks
1 tbsp fresh lemon juice
salt and freshly ground black pepper

1 Bend the asparagus stems, letting them break where they will; discard the tough ends and wash the rest. Cut into 3-cm (one-and-a-quarter-inch) lengths.

2 Cook the asparagus in a little boiling water for three to four minutes, until the stems are only just tender, and then drain.

3 Melt the butter gently in a saucepan without browning it. Put the egg yolks, lemon juice and some seasoning into a food processor or blender and whizz for one minute, until thick.

4 With the machine running, pour in the melted butter in a thin, steady stream, and the sauce will thicken. Allow to stand for a minute or two, then serve while still hot, with the hot asparagus.

4

Exotic Veg

I've interpreted the title of this section loosely The recipes here either use rather exotic ingredients, or else they consist of an unusual mixture, such as garlic, ground almonds and grapes in the White Gazpacho (page 50), so that the overall effect is exotic.

After you've tried the White Gazpacho, taste the Baby Spinach and Summer Berry Salad (page 58) or the Grilled Goats Cheese on Pears with Watercress on (page 72), and then tell me you don't find them intriguing. All are easy to make and full of colour and flavour: a great way to enjoy yourself and virtuously eat the recommended five servings of fruit and vegetables a day.

WHITE GAZPACHO

It's white, it's chilled, it's delicious and it's from Spain – but there the similarity to the red gazpacho we know and love ends. This is a wonderful, piquant mixture of sweet and sour: a heavenly dish on a hot day.

Serves 4
200 g or 8 oz whole almonds
2 slices of bread (white or wholemeal),
  crusts removed
2 garlic cloves, crushed
3 tbsp sherry vinegar or balsamic vinegar
600 ml or 20fl oz ice-water
sea salt and freshly ground black pepper
250 g or 9 oz sweet, green seedless
  grapes, halved

1 Put the almonds into a small saucepan, cover with water and boil for one minute. Drain and slip the skins off the almonds.

2 Put the almonds into a food processor with the bread, garlic and vinegar. Whizz very thoroughly, until the almonds are as fine as you can get them, then add a little water to make a paste and whizz again. Gradually add the rest of the water until you have a gorgeously creamy mixture. Season with salt and pepper. Chill until required.

3 To serve, divide the grapes among four chilled bowls and ladle the soup on top.

WINTER ROAST VEG
WITH HALLOUMI

Roasted vegetables aren't just for summer, as this warming winter mix shows all too deliciously. Halloumi cheese is available from most large supermarkets and makes a particularly attractive topping. Serve this on its own or with some watercress on the side.

Serves 3-4
2 large baking potatoes, scrubbed
2 sweet potatoes, scrubbed
2 large red onions, peeled
2 parsnips, scrubbed
2 large carrots, scrubbed
3-4 tbsp olive oil
salt and freshly ground black pepper
5-6 garlic cloves, peeled and chopped
5-6 sprigs of rosemary, chopped
250 g or 9 oz Halloumi cheese

METHOD

1 Pre-heat the oven to 200°C (400°F or gas mark 6).

2 Cut the potatoes into 1-cm (half-inch) squares and the rest of the vegetables into 2.5-cm (one-inch) squares. Place them all in a roasting tin, add the oil and some salt and pepper and move the vegetables around with your hands so that they're all coated in oil.

3 Put into the oven and bake for 30 minutes. Remove from the oven, stir in the garlic and rosemary, then return to the oven for a further 15 minutes.

4 Drain the Halloumi cheese, and, using a sharp knife, slice it as thinly as you can.

5 Remove the roasting tin of vegetables from the oven and put the slices of Halloumi all over the top, then bake for a further 15 minutes, until the Halloumi is golden brown. Serve at once.

Warm sweet potato salad

Serves 2
2 red-fleshed sweet potatoes, scrubbed
1 tbsp olive oil
200 g or 7 oz feta cheese
1 bunch or packet of watercress, washed
1 handful of black olives
salt and freshly ground black pepper

1 Pre-heat the oven to 200°C (400°F or gas mark 6).

2 Cut the sweet potatoes into 1-cm (half-inch) squares. Place these in a roasting tin with the oil and mix thoroughly. Bake for 30 minutes, until tender and lightly browned.

3 Cut the cheese into cubes to match the sweet potatoes.

4 Put the watercress into a salad bowl, add the hot sweet potatoes, cheese and olives. Season with a little salt and pepper (not too much salt, because of the saltiness of the feta) and serve. The sharpness of the feta cheese and saltiness of the olives contrast perfectly with the sweetness of the potatoes.

BABY SPINACH AND
SUMMER BERRY SALAD

When my friend Annie raved about this salad she'd eaten in Vancouver, Canada, I thought 'Hmm…' But she kept on about it, so I tried it. Then I began to rave, too.

Serves 2-4
1 tbsp raspberry vinegar
2 tbsp olive oil
salt and freshly ground black pepper
1 red onion, finely sliced
100 g or 3^1/$_2$ oz flaked almonds
225 g or 8 oz firm log goats cheese
1 packet baby leaf spinach
225 g or 8 oz summer berries: raspberries,
    strawberries or blueberries, ready to eat

METHOD

1 Mix the raspberry vinegar, olive oil and some salt and pepper in a salad bowl. Add the onion and leave on one side. This can be done in advance if convenient, which allows the onion to soften in the dressing, but it is not essential.

2 Put the flaked almonds in a dry saucepan, stir over the heat for a few minutes until they turn golden, then tip them onto a plate before they over-cook.

3 Cut the goats cheese into bite-size pieces, and grill until nicely browned.

4 Mix the spinach, berries and almonds into the salad bowl, top with the hot goats cheese, and serve at once.

OVEN-BAKED WILD MUSHROOM RISOTTO

I quite like making a risotto in the usual way, as on page 78, but there are times when it's great to let the oven do all the work.

Serves 2-3

30 g or 1 oz packet dried
    porcini mushrooms
600 ml or 20fl oz vegetable stock
    (see page 13)
1 tbsp olive oil
15 g or half an ounce of butter
1 onion, finely chopped
250 g or 9 oz chestnut mushrooms, sliced
2 garlic cloves, chopped
175 g or 6 oz carnaroli or other risotto rice
150 ml or 5fl oz dry Madeira, vermouth
    or sherry
salt and freshly ground black pepper
75 g or 3 oz fresh Parmesan

METHOD

1 Preheat the oven to 150°C (300°F or gas mark 2). Put the porcini and stock into a pan, bring to the boil, then set aside.

2 Heat the oil and butter in a large saucepan, put in the onion and mushrooms; stir and cook gently, uncovered, for 15 to 20 minutes.

3 Add the garlic and rice; stir, then pour in the Madeira, vermouth or sherry and the porcini with all their liquid. Add a teaspoon of salt and a grinding of pepper, bring to the boil, then tip the whole lot into an ovenproof dish and put into the oven, uncovered.

4 Grate two tablespoons of Parmesan cheese and set aside. Shave the rest into flakes with a potato peeler and put into a bowl to go on the table.

5 Bake for 20 minutes, then stir in the two tablespoons of grated Parmesan cheese and bake for a further 15 minutes. Remove from the oven and cover with a clean, folded tea towel for a minute or so, then serve with the rest of the Parmesan.

LEMONY BRAISED VEGETABLES

Make a meal of this by serving with baby
new potatoes, mashed potatoes, cooked
rice, bread, noodles, or for real indulgence,
Gratin Dauphinoise on page 35. This makes
a lot, but if there's any left, it's great cold.

Serves 4
4 tbsp olive oil
1 bay leaf
grated rind and juice of 1 lemon
a good pinch of dried thyme
4 carrots, cut into batons
2 red peppers, deseeded and sliced
1 head of broccoli, cut into florets
200 g or 7 oz mange-tout, halved lengthways
2 tbsp chopped parsley
salt and freshly ground black pepper

1 Put the olive oil into a saucepan with the bay leaf, lemon rind, thyme and 200 ml or 7fl oz water and bring to the boil.

2 Put the carrots into the pan and simmer for 10 minutes, then add the peppers and broccoli and cook for a further five to six minutes, until they're nearly tender; add the mange-tout and cook for a further two to three minutes.

3 Add the lemon juice and parsley. Season with salt and pepper and serve.

GOATS CHEESE IN PUFF
PASTRY WITH CRANBERRIES

Serves 4
350 g or 12 oz ready-rolled puff pastry
2 x 100 g or 3$^{1}/_{2}$ oz firm goats cheese logs
125 g or 4$^{1}/_{2}$ oz cranberry sauce
milk or beaten egg to glaze

1 Preheat the oven to 220°C (425°F or gas mark 7).

2 Roll the pastry a little on a floured surface to make it a bit thinner if you can, then cut it into eight 10-cm (four-inch) circles.

3 Slice each goats cheese in half horizontally. Place a piece on four of the circles, cut-side uppermost so it won't ooze. Put a spoonful of cranberry sauce on top.

4 Brush the edges with water, then put another circle on top of each and press the edges together firmly.

5 Brush with milk or egg, prick the top, place on a baking sheet and bake for 15 minutes, or until golden brown and puffy. Serve hot with a green salad and some baby potatoes.

CRUMBED AVOCADOS
WITH LIME SAUCE

Serves 4
2 almost-ripe avocados
1 tbsp lemon juice
salt and freshly ground black pepper
4 tbsp arrowroot or cornflour
4 tbsp water
75 g or 3 oz dry breadcrumbs
8 tbsp mayonnaise
juice of 1 lime
1 tbsp capers
1 garlic clove, crushed
vegetable oil for, frying

1 Halve, stone and peel the avocados; cut each half into five or six slices and sprinkle with lemon juice, salt and pepper.

2 Mix the arrowroot or cornflower with the water. Dip the pieces of avocado first in this, then into the breadcrumbs.

3 Make the sauce by mixing the mayonnaise, lime juice, capers and garlic. Set aside.

4 Cover the bottom of a frying pan with about 1 cm (half an inch) of vegetable oil; heat. Put in the avocado slices and fry for a couple of minutes on each side, until golden and crisp. Drain on kitchen paper. Serve with the sauce.

GRILLED GOATS CHEESE ON PEARS WITH WATERCRESS

Serves 4
2 tbsp olive oil
15 g or half an ounce of butter
4 ripe pears, peeled, cored and sliced
2 x 225 g or 8 oz firm goats cheese logs
1 packet of watercress
1 tbsp red wine or cider vinegar
salt and freshly ground black pepper

1 Heat one tablespoon of the olive oil and all the butter in a pan; put in the pears, cover and cook gently for about seven minutes, or until tender and lightly browned.

2 Heat the grill to high. Cut the goats cheese in half horizontally. Put the rounds on a lightly greased grill pan and grill for about five minutes, or until lightly browned and melting.

3 Toss the watercress in the remaining tablespoon of oil and the vinegar; season with salt and pepper.

4 Divide the watercress among four plates; arrange the pears over it, then top each plate with a round of goats cheese and serve at once.

5

Spicy Veg

All recipes in this section contain spices in some form, ranging from the hot flavour-burst of fresh chilli, warming ginger and glorious golden saffron to the gentler stimulus of cumin, cardamom, turmeric and cinnamon.

Don't worry if you haven't got shelves full of spices in stock. In fact a few key ones are all you need (see pages 13–14), and you can collect them gradually. Remember, too, that it's *your* dinner you're making, not mine, so please feel free to disagree with me and use more or less flavouring. Or even to change it.

The one thing you do need to do is taste what you're making as you go along, to get it exactly as you like it. Bon appetit!

THAI VEGETABLES
IN COCONUT MILK

Serves 2
1 tbsp oil
1 tbsp Thai red curry paste
1 garlic clove, crushed
1 red pepper, deseeded and chopped
150 g or 5 oz green beans, topped, tailed
and halved
150 g or 5 oz mange-tout, halved lengthways
150 g or 5 oz baby sweetcorn,
halved lengthways
400 ml or 14fl oz can coconut milk
juice of 1 lime
salt and freshly ground black pepper
15 g or half an ounce fresh coriander,
finely chopped

1 Heat the oil in a large saucepan or wok, put in the Thai paste and garlic, stir briefly, then add the red pepper. Cook for four to five minutes, stirring often, then add the beans and cook for a further two to three minutes.

2 Put in the mange-tout and sweetcorn and stir-fry for a minute or two longer.

3 Add the coconut milk, lime juice and salt and pepper to taste. Bring to the boil, sprinkle with the coriander, and serve.

FOOLPROOF SAFFRON RISOTTO

I recommend this served with a leafy salad containing some peppery ingredients such as rocket or watercress.

Serves 4
1 tbsp olive oil
1 celery heart, finely chopped
1 onion, peeled and chopped
2 large garlic cloves, crushed
400 g or 14 oz arborio or other risotto rice
1/4 tsp saffron threads
2 glasses of vermouth or white wine
1,200ml or 40fl oz stock (see page 13)
55 g or 2 oz butter
salt and freshly ground black pepper
125 g or 4 1/2 oz Parmesan, freshly grated

1 Heat the olive oil in a large saucepan; put in the celery and onion. Stir, then cover and cook for seven minutes. Add the garlic, rice and saffron. Stir well, then pour in the vermouth or wine and let it bubble as you stir.

2 Now add a ladleful of the stock, stirring. When it has been absorbed, add another and continue until the rice is tender – about 25 minutes.

3 Stir in the butter, salt and pepper and Parmesan; cover with a folded cloth and leave for a minute or two for them to melt creamily into the rice, then stir with a fork and serve.

TURKISH AUBERGINE PILAF

Serves 4
2 aubergines, sliced lengthways
3 tbsp olive oil
1 onion, peeled and chopped
2 large garlic cloves, sliced
2 tsp cumin seeds
225 g or 8 oz tomatoes, chopped
225 g or 8 oz basmati rice
400 ml or 14fl oz boiling water
salt and freshly ground black pepper
juice of 1 lemon

1 Cut the aubergine halves into slices about 1 cm (half an inch) thick again, so you have four slices from each. Use two tablespoons of the oil to brush the slices, then grill them until golden brown on both sides. Cut into pieces and set aside.

2 In a covered pan, cook the onion in the remaining oil for seven to eight minutes, stirring occasionally. Add the garlic, cumin and tomatoes; cook, uncovered, for about 10 minutes, until any wateriness has gone.

3 Stir the rice into the tomato mixture along with a generous teaspoonful of salt and a grinding of pepper. Pour in the boiling water, cover and leave to cook for 10 minutes.

4 Remove the pan from the heat. Pour the lemon juice on top and then put the aubergines on top of that. Cover and leave to stand, off the heat, for 10 minutes.

5 Mix with a fork, taste and add more seasoning, if necessary, then serve.

Guacamole

This authentic guacamole is best if you can start it about an hour before you want to eat it so that the flavours can blend. Yet it's also fine if you whizz it up at the last minute.

Serves 4
1 small bunch or packet of coriander,
* finely chopped*
4 tomatoes, finely chopped
1 green chilli, deseeded and finely chopped
2 large avocados
salt and freshly ground black pepper

1 Put the coriander, tomatoes and chilli into a bowl. Mix and set aside.

2 Just before serving, halve, skin and stone the avocados. Mash them into the coriander mixture with a fork for a fairly coarse texture, or transfer everything to a food processor and pulse a few times until you have the desired consistency. Season with salt and freshly ground black pepper, and serve.

Quick Korma

Serve this gentle, fragrant korma with some plain, cooked basmati rice and perhaps a little fresh tomato chutney: sliced tomatoes, chopped spring onion and lemon juice.

Serves 2

1 tbsp vegetable oil

1 onion, chopped

1 garlic clove, chopped

2 tsp grated fresh ginger

¼ tsp cinnamon

seeds from 6 cardamom pods

half a tsp turmeric

250 g or 9 oz green beans,
*   trimmed and halved*

250 g or 9 oz broccoli florets

25 g or 1 oz coconut cream

100 g or 3½ oz unsalted cashews

salt and pepper

1-2 tbsp fresh lemon juice

2 tbsp chopped fresh coriander

METHOD

1 In a large covered saucepan, cook the onion in the oil for seven minutes, until tender but not browned. Add the garlic, ginger, cinnamon, cardamom seeds and turmeric; stir for a few seconds, then remove from the heat and set aside.

2 Boil 1 cm (half an inch) of water in another pan; put in the beans and the broccoli. Cover and simmer for about four to five minutes, until they're just tender. Drain, reserving the liquid; measure and, if necessary, make this up to 300 ml (10fl oz). Put the broccoli and beans back in the pan.

3 Put the onion mixture into a food processor or blender with the coconut cream, cashews and reserved water, and whizz into a cream. Season with salt, pepper and lemon juice and pour over the beans and broccoli.

4 Reheat gently, stirring. Check seasoning, sprinkle with the chopped coriander, and serve.

Mushrooms in saffron cream

Creamy and indulgent and *sooo* good. This dish is delicious with quickly cooked basmati rice, and you can add a green salad on the side if you're feeling virtuous. Or you could simply serve it on hot, buttered white toast.

Serves 2
500 g or 1 lb 2 oz button
   chestnut mushrooms
1 tbsp olive oil
15 g or half an ounce of butter
1 garlic clove, crushed
a good pinch of saffron threads
150 ml or 5 fl oz double cream
salt and freshly ground black pepper
a little fresh lemon juice
2 tbsp chopped parsley

1 Wash the mushrooms, halve or quarter as necessary and pat dry on kitchen paper.

2 Heat the oil and butter in a saucepan, put in the garlic, mushrooms and saffron, and cook gently, uncovered, for about four minutes, or until the mushrooms are tender.

3 Stir in the cream. Let it bubble, uncovered, for two to three minutes to thicken slightly.

4 Add the salt, pepper and a few drops of fresh lemon juice to taste. Sprinkle with the chopped parsley, and serve.

PIQUANT ONION TARTS

Serves 4-6
2 tbsp olive oil
4 red onions, sliced
500 g or 1 lb 2 oz ready-made puff pastry
2 tbsp pine nuts
2 tbsp capers
2 tbsp chopped sun-dried tomatoes
2 tbsp chopped pitted black olives
125 g or 4½ oz feta cheese, diced
1 tbsp chopped rosemary (optional)
salt and freshly ground black pepper

1 Preheat the oven to 210°C (425°F or gas mark 7).

2 Heat the oil in a large saucepan. Put in the onions, cover, and cook gently for 15 minutes, stirring occasionally. Remove from the heat.

3 Roll out the pastry on a floured surface and cut into four 15-cm (six-inch) circles; prick with a fork. Put into the fridge to chill briefly.

4 Stir the nuts, capers, tomatoes, olives, cheese and rosemary (if using) into the onions; season. Put the pastry circles on a baking sheet; top with the onion mixture, leaving about 1 cm (half an inch) clear around the edges.

5 Bake for about 15 minutes, or until the pastry is golden and puffed up. Serve at once.

A VEGETARIAN CAESAR

Everyone loves Caesar salad, but if you're vegetarian, you've almost always got to make it yourself, as the restaurant versions usually contain anchovies. It's easy to do; replace fishy flavours with zingy ingredients such as Tabasco and capers, and make gorgeous generous-sized croutons as well.

Serves 2-4
1 small, slim baguette or ficelle
olive oil
4 tbsp good-quality mayonnaise
1 garlic clove, crushed
Tabasco sauce
2 tbsp capers, rinsed and drained
125 g or 4½ oz fresh Parmesan, grated
1 cos lettuce, washed

1 Heat the grill. Cut the baguette into slices about 6 mm (a quarter of an inch) thick. Brush both sides with olive oil and grill until golden on both sides, turning them over when the first side is done.

2 Meanwhile, mix the mayonnaise with the garlic and add some Tabasco sauce; shake some drops in, then taste to get the right heat. Stir in the capers and half the cheese.

3 Tear the lettuce into rough, largish pieces and put these into a salad bowl. Add the mayonnaise mixture, the croutons and the remaining Parmesan, mix gently, and serve.

HOT, SPICY, BAKED AVOCADOS

Serves 2-4
1 onion, peeled and chopped
1 tbsp olive oil
1 chilli, deseeded and chopped
half a tsp curry powder
2 large, ripe avocados
100 g or 3½ oz roasted cashew nuts
  roughly chopped
100 g or 3½ oz Gruyère cheese, diced
2 tbsp chopped parsley
2 tbsp sherry
salt and freshly ground black pepper
4 tbsp fresh Parmesan cheese, grated

1 Preheat the oven to 200°C (400°F or gas mark 6).

2 Fry the onion in the oil for seven minutes, then add the chilli and curry powder and fry for a further two to three minutes.

3 Halve and stone the avocados, then scoop out the flesh with a teaspoon and chop it.

4 Combine the avocado with the onion mixture, along with the nuts, Gruyère, parsley, sherry and seasoning.

5 Pile the mixture back into the avocado skins, top with the grated Parmesan and bake for 10 to 15 minutes until golden brown and heated through.

6

Pasta Veg

Most of these recipes combine pasta and vegetables. There are a few particularly decadent ones which consist mainly of pasta, cream and cheese, so you can indulge yourself completely. And you can always add a bit of virtue in the form of a fresh, leafy, green salad on the side.

In each recipe I've suggested the type of pasta that I think goes particularly well with the ingredients, but please feel free to use other types if you prefer, or haven't got the type mentioned. All these pasta dishes feed two people generously.

FETTUCINE WITH LEMON CREAM

Serves 2
250 g or 9 oz fettucine
150 ml or 5fl oz double cream
finely grated rind and juice of 1 lemon
salt and freshly ground black pepper
1 tbsp olive oil
fresh Parmesan, grated or flaked, to serve

1 Bring a large saucepan of water to the boil, put in the pasta and boil for about six to eight minutes (or according to the pasta packet instructions) until it's al dente.

2 Meanwhile, put the cream into a small saucepan with the grated lemon rind and some salt and pepper.

3 Drain the pasta and return it to the pasta pan to keep warm, with the tablespoonful of olive oil and some salt and pepper.

4 Bring the cream to the boil, then remove from the heat and stir in the lemon juice. Pour this over the pasta and turn it gently so that it all gets coated. Serve immediately, with a bowl of Parmesan cheese and a green salad.

Fettucine with pecorino, cream and truffle oil

Serves 2
250 g or 9 oz fettucine
150 ml or 5fl oz double cream
125 g or 4½ oz hard pecorino cheese, grated
3 tbsp truffle oil
salt and freshly ground black pepper
fresh Parmesan, grated or flaked to serve

1 Bring a large saucepan of water to the boil, put in the pasta and boil for about six to eight minutes (according to the pasta packet instructions) until it's al dente.

2 Meanwhile, put the cream into a small saucepan with the pecorino and set aside.

3 Drain the pasta and return it to the pasta pan to keep warm. Add the truffle oil and toss well, seasoning with some salt and pepper.

4 Bring the cream to the boil, then pour into the pasta. Toss the pasta until it's thoroughly coated. Serve immediately with a bowl of Parmesan cheese and a green salad.

PENNE WITH MINT PESTO, PEAS AND BROAD BEANS

Serves 2
250 g or 9 oz penne or other short pasta
125 g or 4½ oz freshly shelled or frozen peas
125 g or 4½ oz small freshly shelled or
   frozen broad beans
1 tbsp mint, roughly chopped
salt and freshly ground black pepper
Parmesan, flaked or grated, to serve (optional)

For the mint pesto:
1 small bunch of mint, stalks removed
1 garlic clove, crushed
2 tbsp olive oil

1 Bring a large saucepan of water to the boil. Put in the pasta and boil until it's almost, but not quite, tender. Add the peas and broad beans and cook for a further two to three minutes, until the pasta is al dente and the peas and beans are done – they take practically no cooking. Drain and return to the pan.

2 Make the mint pesto by whizzing the mint, garlic and olive oil in a food processor until you have a green purée. Stir this into the pasta mixture, along with the roughly chopped mint, and season to taste.

3 Serve immediately, with some Parmesan scattered on top if desired.

PAPPARDELLE
WITH WILD MUSHROOMS

By 'wild' mushrooms, I mean whatever you can lay your hands on: a supermarket bag of 'wild' mushrooms, if available. Or a base of chestnut mushrooms plus any interesting extras you can find – maybe a few shiitakes, some morels, ceps or even chanterelles if you're very lucky (or very rich).

Serves 2
30 g or 1 oz porcini mushrooms
15 g or half an ounce of butter
olive oil
1 garlic clove, crushed
500 g or 1 lb 2 oz mixed 'wild' mushrooms,
  sliced as necessary
a sprig of thyme
2-3 tbsp double cream (optional)
salt and freshly ground black pepper
grated nutmeg
250 g or 9 oz pappardelle
fresh Parmesan, flaked or grated (optional)

Method

1 Put the porcini into a small bowl, just cover with a little boiling water and leave to soak for 20 minutes or so.

2 In a saucepan, melt the butter with a tablespoonful of the oil, add the garlic; stir. Then add the wild mushrooms and thyme, stir, and leave to cook until any liquid which comes from the mushrooms has boiled away.

3 Add the porcini mushrooms and their liquid and cook again until the liquid has more or less disappeared. Stir in the cream, if using, and season to taste with salt, pepper and nutmeg.

4 Meanwhile, bring a large saucepan of water to the boil, put in the pasta and boil until al dente. Drain and return to the pan.

5 If you want to serve the wild mushrooms mixed with the pasta, add it now, and toss the pasta. If you'd rather serve the pasta with the mushrooms on top, add a tablespoonful of olive oil to the pasta, toss, then serve the pasta in bowls and spoon the mushrooms over. Hand around the Parmesan separately.

Spaghetti with chilli-tomato sauce and black olives

This is such a quick and easy sauce for pasta. You can make it in not much more time than it takes to open a jar – certainly by the time the water has boiled and the pasta has cooked. And it tastes so much nicer.

Serves 2
2 tbsp olive oil
1 onion, finely chopped
1 garlic clove, crushed
425 g or 15 oz can chopped tomatoes
¼ tsp dried chilli flakes
salt and freshly ground black pepper
200 g or 7 oz spaghetti
a handful of black olives
Parmesan cheese, flaked or grated,
   to serve (optional)

Method

1 To start the sauce: cook the onion in one tablespoonful of the olive oil in a covered saucepan for seven minutes, until tender but not browned, stirring from time to time. Add the garlic, tomatoes and chilli flakes and leave to simmer, uncovered, for 10 to 15 minutes, until thick. Season with salt and pepper.

2 Meanwhile, bring a large saucepan of water to the boil, put in the pasta and boil until al dente, following packet directions. Drain and return to the pan; season.

3 If you want to serve the sauce mixed with the pasta, add it now, along with the olives, and toss the pasta.

4 If you'd rather serve the pasta with the sauce on top, add a tablespoonful of olive oil to the pasta, toss, then serve the pasta in bowls, pour on the tomato sauce and top with some olives. Hand round the Parmesan separately.

PENNE WITH TOMATO SAUCE AND AUBERGINES

Serves 2
1 large aubergine, quartered lengthways
3-4 tbsp olive oil
1 onion, finely chopped
1 garlic clove, crushed
425 g or 15 oz can chopped tomatoes
1/4 tsp dried chilli flakes
salt and freshly ground black pepper
250 g or 9 oz penne
fresh basil
freshly ground black pepper
Parmesan cheese, flaked to serve (optional)

1 Brush the aubergine quarters with olive oil, spread on a grill pan and grill until browned on both sides, turning them halfway through. Then cut the slices into smaller stumpy pieces.

2 Cook the onion in a tablespoonful of oil in a covered saucepan for seven minutes, stirring occasionally, until tender but not brown. Add the garlic, tomatoes and chilli flakes; simmer uncovered for 10 to 15 minutes, until thick. Season with salt and pepper.

3 Bring a large saucepan of water to the boil, put in the pasta and boil until al dente, following packet directions. Drain and return to the pan; season.

4 Mix the sauce with the pasta and toss. To serve with the sauce on top, add a tablespoonful of olive oil to the pasta, toss, then serve in bowls. Pour on the tomato sauce and top with slices of roast aubergine and flakes of Parmesan.

Rigatoni with artichoke hearts and pine nuts

Serves 2
1 large purple onion, fairly finely sliced
2 tbsp olive oil
2 garlic cloves, sliced
2 good-sized courgettes, cut into
   1-cm or half-inch dice
2 tomatoes, roughly chopped
6 artichoke hearts in oil, drained
sea salt and freshly ground black pepper
250 g or 9 oz rigatoni
2 tbsp pine nuts, toasted
1 tbsp torn basil leaves
fresh Parmesan cheese, flaked or grated

1 Toast the pine nuts under a hot grill for one to two minutes. Remove and set aside.

2 In a covered saucepan, cook the onion in a tablespoonful of the oil for seven minutes, until tender (not brown), stirring occasionally. Add the garlic, courgettes and tomatoes and cook uncovered for about five minutes, until the courgettes are tender. Add the artichoke hearts. Season with salt and pepper.

3 Cook the pasta according to the packet directions. Drain and return to the pasta pan; add the courgette mixture, pine nuts and basil and season to taste.

4 Dish out onto warm plates, scatter with Parmesan, and serve.

FARFALLE WITH ONION, SPINACH AND RICOTTA

Serves 2
3-4 tbsp olive oil
1 onion, finely chopped
1 garlic clove, crushed
100 g or 3 1/2 oz baby leaf spinach
salt and freshly ground black pepper
grated nutmeg
250 g or 9 oz farfalle
125 g or 4 1/2 oz ricotta cheese
fresh Parmesan cheese, grated
flaked Parmesan cheese to serve (optional)

1 In a covered saucepan, cook the onion in one tablespoonful of olive oil for seven minutes, until tender but not brown, stirring occasionally. Add the garlic and spinach; cook for a minute or two longer, until the spinach has wilted. Season with salt, pepper and nutmeg. Set aside.

2 Meanwhile, bring a large saucepan of water to the boil, put in the pasta and boil until al dente, following packet directions. Drain and return to the pasta pan. Stir in the ricotta and the spinach mixture. Toss gently, check seasoning, then serve into bowls and top with grated Parmesan.

Linguine with Gorgonzola

One of the simplest and quickest pasta dishes, and wonderfully rich and tasty. Serve it with a simple leafy salad which includes some peppery leaves such as rocket or watercress. Other semi-soft cheeses can be used instead of Gorgonzola; Danish Blue is a cheaper option but still tasty.

Serves 2
200 g or 7 oz linguine
175 g or 6 oz Gorgonzola cheese
25 g or 1 oz butter
freshly ground black pepper

1 Bring a large saucepan of water to the boil, put in the pasta and boil until al dente, following the packet directions. Drain and return to the pan.

2 Crumble the Gorgonzola into the pan on top of the hot pasta and add the butter; grind in some pepper. Toss the pasta gently so that it all gets coated with the melting cheese and butter. Serve at once.

Summer penne

Serves 2
1 red pepper
1 gold pepper
125 g or 4½ oz cherry tomatoes
250 g or 9 oz penne
125 g or 4½ oz asparagus tips
1 tbsp olive oil
1 garlic clove, crushed
2-3 sprigs of basil, torn
salt and freshly ground black pepper
fresh Parmesan, flaked

1 Halve and deseed the peppers. Place cut-side down on a grill pan along with the cherry tomatoes. Grill for about 10 minutes, or until the peppers are tender and blackened in places. Cool, then cut the peppers into chunky pieces.

2 Start cooking the pasta, following packet directions. About three to four minutes before the pasta is done, add the asparagus, so it will be just tender when the pasta is ready.

3 Drain the pasta and asparagus and put it back in the pan; add the oil, garlic and salt and pepper to taste, and mix gently but thoroughly, then stir in the peppers and tomatoes. Serve topped with basil leaves, and Parmesan cheese if desired.

7

Puddings

Pudding is often the best bit of the meal and should not be ignored, especially when you are spoiling yourself. The recipes here, such as the Super-fast Ice-cream (page 152), are really very easy, as are most of the fruity puddings. The White Chocolate Cheesecake (page 154) and the Chocolate Torte (page 146) as well as the Fast and Wonderful Chocolate Brownies (page 124) are also a lot of fun to make, and the look of pleasure on people's faces when you produce them makes them worth the effort. While some are downright indulgent, others are healthy and won't pile on the pounds.

Fast and wonderful
chocolate brownies

Just measuring, melting and stirring are all that's required to make these. Get them into the oven before you sit down to eat and they'll be ready for afterwards, all warm and gooey from the oven. Serve with cream, ice-cream or thick, natural yoghurt.

Makes 15
100 g or 3½ oz *walnut pieces, or*
  roughly chopped pecans
100 g or 3½ oz *butter, in rough pieces*
100 g or 3½ oz *plain chocolate,*
  broken into pieces
225 g or 8 oz *light-brown sugar*
2 *eggs*
55 g or 2 oz *self-raising flour*

Method

1 Preheat the oven to 180°C (350°F or gas mark 4). Line a 20-cm (eight-inch) square tin with non-stick paper.

2 Put the nuts onto a baking tray and bake for around six to eight minutes, until they're golden and smell wonderful. Set aside.

3 In a saucepan, melt the butter and chocolate over a gentle heat. Remove from the heat and stir in the sugar, eggs and flour. Beat together until smooth, then stir in the nuts.

4 Pour into the tin and bake for about 30 minutes; the brownies will be firm at the edges and still soft in the middle. Cool for a few minutes, then cut into slices. Remove from the tin with a spatula.

BAKED APRICOTS
WITH STRAWBERRIES

So often, apricots are disappointingly hard. But if you bake them in the oven and then mix them with another seasonal fruits – strawberries, for example – the result is quite delightful.

Serves 4
500 g or 1 lb 2 oz apricots
125 g or 4½ oz caster sugar
juice of 1 orange
500 g or 1 lb 2 oz ripe strawberries

1 Preheat the oven to 180°C (350°F or gas mark 4).

2 Wash, halve and stone the apricots, then put them into a casserole. Sprinkle with the sugar and pour on the orange juice. Cover with a lid or foil and bake for about 45 minutes, or until the apricots are tender.

3 Wash and hull the strawberries, then halve or slice them, depending on their size, and add to the apricots.

4 Serve at once, or leave to cool.

Rhubarb crumble

Serves 4
900 g or 2 lb rhubarb
175 g or 6 oz caster sugar
175 g or 6 oz plain flour
125 g or 4½ oz unsalted butter

1 Preheat the oven to 200°C (400°F or gas mark 6).

2 Wash the rhubarb. Top, tail, remove any tough strings and cut it into 1-cm (half-inch) lengths. Put the pieces into a shallow casserole dish and sprinkle with half the sugar.

3 Rub the butter into the sugar until it forms a crumbly mixture, then stir in the rest of the sugar; you can do this by hand or in a food processor, but don't whizz it so much that it all combines. Then stir in one tablespoonful of water to keep it crumbly.

4 Put the crumble mixture evenly on top of the rhubarb, then bake for about 35 minutes, until crisp and golden.

SUMMER FRUIT FOOL

Serves 4
225 g or 8 oz strawberries, stalks removed
225 g or 8 oz raspberries
225 g or 8 oz blueberries or blackberries
75 g-125 g or 3-4½ oz caster sugar
300 ml or 10fl oz double cream, or
  half cream and half Greek yoghurt,
  or just yoghurt

1 Simply put all the fruits into a saucepan with the sugar and heat gently for about five minutes until the juices run. Remove from the heat and set aside to cool.

2 If you're using some yoghurt with (or without) the cream, stir this in when the fruit is cool. Whisk the cream until it's light and thick, then fold it into the cooled fruit mixture. It doesn't have to be completely smooth; some purple-red drifts of fruit are part of the charm.

Ginger-baked Pears

Serves 4
4 ripe pears
55 g or 2 oz caster sugar
1-2 lumps of preserved ginger in
  syrup, chopped, and 2 tbsp of the syrup

1 Preheat the oven to 200°C (400°F or gas mark 6).

2 Peel, core and slice the pears. Put them into a casserole dish and mix in the caster sugar, preserved ginger and syrup.

3 Bake for about 30 minutes, until they're tender, stirring them once or twice during cooking to make sure they're cooking evenly in the juices.

4 Serve hot or cold, with some thick yoghurt, cream or vanilla ice-cream.

PLUMS AND CREAM OR YOGHURT

Often, lots of plums in the shops are not always as sweet and ripe as you'd like. Cook them quickly with some sugar, however, and they become juicy and lovely, especially when served with thick cream.

Serves 4
750 g or 1 lb 10 oz plums, any colour
125 g or 4½ oz caster sugar
double cream or thick yoghurt, to serve

1 Wash the plums, then put them, with the water still clinging to them, into a saucepan and add the sugar.

2 Place the saucepan over a moderate heat and leave to cook gently for about 10 minutes, until they're tender and beginning to collapse.

3 Serve hot, warm or cold.

AN EXOTIC FRUIT SALAD

Serves 4
2 sweet, juicy oranges
1 large, ripe mango (or 2 small)
1 large, ripe pawpaw
2 ripe kiwi fruit
225 g or 8 oz sweet purple grapes
2 passion fruit, wrinkled and heavy

1 Holding the oranges over a bowl, cut off the peel and pith thickly, slicing round and round and letting any juice drip into the bowl. Then cut the juicy segments and put into the bowl. Squeeze any remaining juice out of the remains of the orange, then discard.

2 Peel and slice the mango, pawpaw and kiwi fruit and add to the bowl along with the halved grapes.

3 Finally, cut the passion fruit in half, scoop out the speckled contents, and add.

Pancakes or Crêpes

We call them pancakes in my house, and when I make them, everyone's face lights up. I prepare them thick or thin as requested, but all from one batch of mixture. I like these best with sugar and lemon, but some like warmed golden syrup, too. It's probably a good thing for my wardrobe that I don't get the urge to make them very often.

Makes about 10
125 g or 4½ oz plain flour
a pinch of salt
2 eggs, beaten
4 tbsp melted butter
350 ml or 12fl oz milk and water, mixed
    half and half
caster sugar and lemon wedges, to serve

METHOD

1 Sift the flour and salt into a bowl; make a well in the middle and pour in the egg and one tablespoonful of the butter (the rest is for frying the pancakes). Mix together, then pour in some of the milk and water. Continue adding and beating – you can use an electric mixer or even do the whole thing in a food processor – until you have a smooth batter.

2 Pancake tradition dictates that you should allow this mixture to stand for a while, but as I've never found that it makes much difference, feel free to go straight ahead to the next step.

3 Brush a small frying pan with some of the melted butter, and set over a medium heat until a drop of water sizzles immediately when flicked into the pan.

4 Pour in a ladleful of batter and swirl it over the pan. To make a thin pancake, pour any excess back into the bowl. Loosen the edges with a palette knife as the pancake cooks, and when the underside is set and lightly browned, flip the pancake over and cook the other side, which will take only a few seconds. Lift it out onto a plate and serve at once, or keep piling them up on the plate until they're all done.

Instant raspberry ice-cream

If you've got a food processor, this is an almost magical dish that you can make any time. All you need is a packet of frozen raspberries in your freezer, a carton of cream and some sugar. You can also make a fabulous non-dairy version using soya 'cream' which you can get at most health shops and probably at some supermarkets.

Serves 4
275 g or 9½ oz frozen raspberries
75 g or about 3 oz caster sugar
300 ml or 10fl oz single cream

1 Put the frozen raspberries, straight out of the freezer, into the food processor.

2 Add the sugar and cream and whizz. In a few seconds, you'll have a thick ice-cream.

3 Scrape down the edges a couple of times and whizz again briefly, if necessary, to get an even mix, then serve immediately.

CHOCOLATE TORTE

You don't need a lot of fancy ingredients such as crushed amaretti biscuits and liquid glucose to make a fabulous chocolate torte. Here's my version. Incidentally, the chocolate topping also works with soya cream if you want to make a stunning non-dairy torte.

Serves 8
250 g or 9 oz digestive biscuits
125 g or 4½ oz butter, melted
200 g or 7 oz plain chocolate,
*   preferably with 70% cocoa solids*
600 ml or 20 fl oz double cream
extra whipped or pouring cream, to serve

1 Crush the biscuits in a food processor or with a rolling pin, then mix with the melted butter and press into the base of a 20-cm (eight-inch) springform cake tin.

2 Break the chocolate into pieces, put into a bowl and set over boiling water to melt. Let it cool slightly while you whip the cream, then pour the chocolate into the cream and fold the two together until combined. If using soya cream, pour this into the melted chocolate and simply whisk until thick.

3 Spoon the chocolate mixture on top of the crumb crust, level the top and put into the fridge to set. Best when thoroughly set after being in the fridge for a while. You can even leave it there overnight.

CHOCOLATE SAUCE

I love to pour this hot sauce over cold vanilla ice-cream. The sauce hardens on contact to make an instant 'choc ice' – childish, maybe, but such comfort food. This sauce also turns ordinary sliced bananas into a fancy pudding, and can be used as a sort of fondue into which you can dip strawberries. Now *that's* indulgence.

Serves 4
200 g or 8 oz plain chocolate,
  preferably with 70% cocoa solids
2 tbsp single cream

ɪ Break the chocolate into pieces, put into a saucepan, pour in the cream and set the pan over a gentle heat until the chocolate has melted, stirring often. Use at once.

Apple tarte tatin

Put this into the oven before dinner, then it's ready for afterwards. You'll need a 20-cm (eight-inch) tart tin or special tarte tatin dish.

Serves 4
325 g or 11½ oz ready-rolled puff pastry
juice of half a lemon
5 medium Cox apples
40 g or 1½ oz butter
40 g or 1½ oz sugar
cream or crème fraîche, to serve

1 Preheat the oven to 200°C (400°F or gas mark 6.

2 Roll the pastry on a floured surface to make it a bit thinner, then cut a circle 1 cm (half an inch) bigger than the top of the tin.

3 Peel and quarter the apples and sprinkle with the lemon juice. Melt the butter in a pan and add the apples and sugar. Cook over a high heat for about six minutes, until the apples are slightly browned.

4 Put the apples, round side down, into your cake tin and scrape in all the gooey juice from the pan, too.

5 Put the pastry on top, tucking it down into the apples at the sides. Prick the pastry, then bake for 20 minutes.

6 To serve, loosen the edges with a knife, then invert over a plate. The apples will be on top. Leave to settle for a couple of minutes before serving.

SUPER-FAST ICE-CREAM

If you put this into a shallow dish in the freezer, you can have some ice-cream in about an hour, so it's quite feasible for a quick meal. It's over-sweet, over-rich and wonderful comfort food. Everyone adores it. This recipe makes a lot, but it will keep in the freezer.

Serves 8-10
600 ml or 20fl oz double or whipping cream
400 ml or 14fl oz can skimmed
*   condensed milk*

1 Whisk the cream until soft peaks form. Use an electric whisk for speed and ease, although you can do it by hand.

2 Add the condensed milk to the cream and whisk again until combined.

3 Tip into a suitable container – a rigid plastic box is ideal – and freeze until firm.

WHITE CHOCOLATE CHEESECAKE

This is pure decadence, and unbelievably easy to make. It's wonderful just as it is, but the lily can be very happily gilded by serving it with warm chocolate sauce (see page 148), or some fresh raspberries.

Serves 6-8
175 g or 6 oz digestive biscuits
75 g or about 3 oz butter
300 g or 10 oz white chocolate
250 g or 9 oz virtually fat-free quark or
other smooth, low-fat white cheese
300 ml or 10fl oz double cream
a little dark chocolate, to decorate

METHOD

1 Crush the biscuits with a rolling pin or food processor.

2 In a medium-size saucepan, melt the butter, then add the crushed crumbs and mix. Press into the base of a 23-cm (nine-inch) springform cake tin. Cool in the fridge or freezer while you make the topping.

3 Break the chocolate into pieces, and put these into a china or glass bowl and melt in the microwave, or in a glass bowl over a saucepan of boiling water.

4 Put the quark or other cheese into a large bowl and whisk in the melted chocolate.

5 Whisk the double cream until it's stiff, then fold into the chocolate mixture. Spoon on top of the crumb base and smooth the top level with a palette knife.

6 Chill until firm. This will take at least an hour in the fridge, or you can speed up the process by putting it into the freezer for about 30 minutes.

7 Slip a knife around the edges of the tin and remove the cheesecake. Decorate with some flakes of chocolate; make these by running a swivel-bladed potato peeler down the length of a bar of plain chocolate. Serve at once.

Index